How to Answer Flight Attendant Interview Questions

JOSEPH BELOTTI

Questions or Comments? Email us: support@airlinecareer.com or visit our website: http://www.airlinecareer.com. Product names, brands, and other trademarks referred to within this book are the property of their respective trademark holders. Unless otherwise specified, no association between the author and any trademark holder is expressed or implied. Use of a term in this book should not be regarded as affecting the validity of any trademark, registered trademark, or service mark.

ISBN 9781973296843

TABLE OF CONTENTS

1 Types of Interview Questions

Thank you for your recent purchase of *"How to Answer Flight Attendant Interview Questions,"* from AirlineCareer.com. We are sure that you will find it informative and will prepare you thoroughly for any type of question you may encounter at your flight attendant pre-employment interview. Since only about 1 out of every 100 applicants is ultimately hired as a flight attendant, interview preparation is extremely important. Another point to remember is that if you are rejected by an airline, you will typically need to wait six to twelve months before you are allowed to reapply. Proper interview preparation will help ensure that you get it right the first time around.

Below you will find virtually every flight attendant interview question imaginable. We have organized the interview questions into several key categories; there are questions on job history, education, company, job description, in-flight scenarios, relocation, reliability, self-analysis, communication, and behavior. For quick navigation to each category and for later review, you can use the chapter list in the Table of Contents on the first page of this book. For every question, there is a recommended answer. Although our recommended answers sometimes won't lend themselves well to your particular situation, we give you more than enough information to create your own unique and persuasive responses.

Every question asked during an interview is aimed at determining your suitability for a flight attendant career. There are no right or wrong answers, but in the eyes of an interviewer, some answers are better than others. Your understanding of the duties and responsibilities and desirable qualities of a flight attendant will help you answer these questions most effectively.

> Important: *The questions asked during your interview(s) probably won't be the exact questions listed here; they should, however, be very close. Regardless of the particular phraseology, the underlying answer the interviewer is seeking will be the same.*

You should follow these general guidelines when answering all interview questions:

- Speak slowly and methodically when answering each question.

- Make sure you understand each question fully before composing your answer; a short pause is fully acceptable.

- Do not be too long-winded; try not to exceed 2 minutes for each answer.

- Tell a story with each answer. Be very specific, using dates and names (if appropriate). Your story should have a beginning, middle, and end.

- Do not memorize a scripted answer for each question; it will become obvious to the interviewer. Instead, write down several key points that you want to cover for each question and review them before the interview.

- Always relate your answers to the duties and responsibilities and desirable qualities of a flight attendant.

- If you are unsure of the answer to a question, be honest and say so; do not try to bluff the interviewer.

- Speak with confidence, using proper grammar at all times.

- Know what questions you are going to ask the interviewer ahead of time.

- Never answer a question with one word, even if the interviewer asks you, for example, to describe yourself in one word. Always elaborate and explain "why."

2 Questions on Job History

An interviewer asks job history questions in order to determine your level of reliability, patience, flexibility, punctuality, conscientiousness and commitment in the workplace; these are extremely important traits of a successful flight attendant.

Chima focused more on sales than guest satisfaction so I switched to EV's because their culture is centered solely on the guests' experience. as a server @ chima?

Why did you leave your last position? Why are you leaving your present position?

Always remember to answer this type of question in a positive manner. Emphasize how happy you are with your present (or past) employer, but how a flight attendant career has always been a personal goal. Talk about all the positive aspects of your past or present position and how your duties relate to the <u>duties of a flight attendant</u>. Do not say anything negative about your previous employer.

More opportunities for growth. which is actually one of the many things I admire about Delta.

- **Is there anything you would like to change in your previous (or present) position?**

A good answer would focus on your desire for increased responsibility and more contact with the public. Be specific.

- In almost 3 years of working for EV's, I have maintained positive reviews from guests' satisfaction surveys. I have not once had a single guest complaint or bad review.

- **What was your greatest contribution at your previous (or present) position?**

I have contributed to the restaurant's overall standings & rating. I've also created loyalty by having "regulars" who always come back to see me

Even if you enjoyed many accomplishments at your previous employer, only talk about the ones that relate directly to the flight

4

attendant position. If you received an award for outstanding customer service, tell the story (in detail). If you went out of your way to solve a problem, talk about it. If you dig deep enough, you are sure to find a project or accomplishment that would be relevant to the flight attendant duties, responsibilities, and traits the interviewer is seeking.

Both my former & current employers would say that

- **What would your former (or present) employer say about you?** *SELL IT w/ a list of adjectives!*

I am a reliable + punctual employee who they can always count on because I always look for opportunities to help the team

I'm flexible.
positive Here is your chance to shine given your understanding of the flight attendant position. Make sure you refer to yourself using as many of
problem solver the desirable qualities of a flight attendant as possible, such as
warm "reliable," "friendly," "outgoing," "patient," "flexible,"
genuine "conscientious," and "punctual." Give specific examples of each

- **What was the one thing you disliked the most at your previous (or current) job?** *I wish there were more opportunities for growth.*

Here is another example of a question that attempts to get you to answer negatively. Any negative comments about your employer will be construed as a dislike for rules and regulations, or even work itself. Rather than answering negatively, turn this question around and answer it positively. You might talk about your position as a telemarketer and how you wished you could have personally met all of your customers whose voices were so familiar to you; this shows your strong interest and desire to work face-to-face with the public. Another way to answer this question is to talk about your office pet peeves: perhaps you are bothered by people who do not promptly respond to your voicemail or email messages? Talk about how you always answer your customers' voicemail, text and email messages promptly; this will show you are a conscientious worker.

No more than 2 times last year due to the common cold, flu, sore throat cough, etc.

How many days were you out sick from work last year?

This question will require an honest answer, because the company will find out sooner or later (during the background check) if you used excessive sick days. If you only missed work a few times due to common illnesses (like colds and the flu), you should openly share this information. Explain how you felt that the company had more to lose if you came to work and spread your sickness to other employees. If you continued to work at home when you were sick, this is an important point to communicate; it shows you are very responsible, productive, and conscientious. If you used an excessive number of sick days for injury or medical problems, explain (in detail) the nature of the problem and how you and your employer dealt with it. Do not elaborate too much on an injury that might preclude you from performing the duties of a flight attendant, such as a chronic back problem.

Serving = carrying heavy dishes requires strength. Walking all around the restaurt at a fast pace on busy nights for anywhere from 5 to 7 hrs straight w/o a break

- **What is the most physically demanding job you ever had?**

This answer can focus on a project you were involved in at work, but does not necessarily have to be job-related. Examples could include working to help build a homeless shelter, delivering and raising a baby,

Serving def requires physical strength + tons of energy to endure the long + busy shifts.

assisting as a camp counselor for special needs children, caring for a senior citizen, training for and running a marathon, etc. Be sure your example relates well to the flight attendant position.

- **Have you ever been involved in a work stoppage?** NO

This is not a common question, but nevertheless could be asked. The interviewer is trying to determine whether you have ever been a member of a union or if you have an understanding of what it means to be a member of a union. Be brief on the answer to this type of question, since it is sensitive in nature. Do not elaborate on the merits of union affiliation and employee solidarity or the interviewer might think you are rebellious and capable of causing problems at the airline.

3 Questions on Education

Interviewers often ask questions about education, even though much of the information is already listed on your resume and application. These types of questions are asked in order for the interviewer to determine your level of motivation and ambition. Since training is an important part of a flight attendant's job, success in your educational pursuits can indicate how well you will perform during new-hire and annual recurrent training.

- **What was your grade point average? Your major?** *3.5*

We recommend on our website that you not include your grade point average on your resume, unless it was extremely high (above 3.5). If it was average or above average, it should not be a problem. If it was low, you will need to do some explaining. The interviewer will want to know whether your performance was affected by other factors, like keeping a full-time job or participating as a member of a varsity sports team. Be honest about whether your performance would have been better without these obstacles.

- **Why did you choose your major?** *Intended to major in Communication*

Do not say anything about choosing a major because it was easy. Also, do not speak negatively about your major. Show your sincere interest in the subject matter of your major and how it relates to your life and job. Also, do not ever say that you could not find a job in a field relating to your major, so you are applying to be a flight attendant! Every major relates in some way to the flight attendant position. Be creative in your answer.

- **Who paid for your college education?** *Full-ride academic scholarship to a 4-yr university*

If you worked your way through college or were part of a work-study program, this is important to discuss; this shows ambition, drive and initiative. Similarly, if you took out student loans to fund your college education, be sure to talk about this as well; this shows you are a financially responsible person. If your parents paid for school, talk about how it was a tremendous sacrifice for them and how you hope someday you will be able to give them something in return (like free travel benefits!)

- **Did you work while in school?** *Yes, full time at my very first job at a restaurt when I 18, shortly after graduating*

This is a variation of the above question and can be answered in the *H.S.* same way. *which is why I was unable to maintain a 3.5 gpa in college so after my second semester the school had to take away my scholarship.*

4. Questions on the Company

These questions are asked in order to determine your enthusiasm for the company. Interviewers want to find out if you did some basic research on the company. An applicant who is knowledgeable about the airline he or she is interviewing with shows initiative, maturity, and resourcefulness.

- **Can you give me any names and positions of the management team of our airline (e.g., President, CEO, etc.)?** CEO → Ed Bastian
  Founder → C. E. Woolman
  Glen Hauenstein → PRESIDENT

Go to the individual airline company websites and learn the names and titles of all of the members of the senior management team. Anything additional known about the team should be stated here as well (e.g. accomplishments at the airline or at a previous company, awards received, etc.).

- **Do you know anything about our route structure?**

Delta celebrated 90 yrs since our very first flight in 1929

Study the route structure as listed in the airline company website. It is also a good idea to study the route map, either on the airline's web site or in the airline's online flight schedule. You do not need to know specific city pairs, but you should know the general airline route structure (Northeast, Northwest, South, Midwest, Europe, Caribbean, etc.). It would also be impressive if you knew the approximate number of destinations the airline serves (also available on the company website).

- We serve 319 destinations in 55 countries
- 80,000 employees world-wide
- We serve 200 million customers a year.

- **Why did you choose this particular airline?**

This should be an easy question for you to answer if you have done your "homework" in researching the airline(s). No doubt you are aware of the pluses and minuses of every airline. In your answer, explain how you did your research on each airline and talk about all of the pluses for the airline you are interviewing with, but go easy on the minuses.

- **Do you know what types of airplanes we fly?**

Airline company websites usually provide you with the total number of aircraft in the fleet in addition to the specific types of aircraft flown. Use our Useful Links section in the Appendix for further research on each type of aircraft, although you probably won't need to know anything beyond the basic type of aircraft.

- **Have you interviewed with any other airlines?**

This does not need to be an overly detailed answer. If you have interviewed with any other airlines, say so. Do not try to explain your airline priorities or say anything derogatory about other airlines you have interviewed with. You can discuss (briefly) your interview experience and status at each airline.

- **Do you have any questions about this airline?**

This question is usually asked at the close of an interview. You can ask questions about the company or flight attendant position (or both).

Review the "About Us" section of the company website and jot down a few questions you would like to ask. Interviewers like questions that show you have a basic understanding of the company. You can ask questions about the company's future growth plans or fleet plan, etc. It is not a bad idea to ask an intelligent question you already know the answer to; this will make you look very well-informed.

- I read in an article that Delta is hiring 3,000 flight attendants for 2020, as opposed to previous years where only 1000 positions were available. Do you know the reason for such high demand this particular year?

- How will my performance as a F.A. be evaluated?

- After finishing the 6 weeks of training, will there be continuous training that we must keep up w/ in order to stay in compliance w/ Delta's policies/procedures?

- What's the #1 advice you would give to someone who gets hired?

- What's the #1 most important quality you think a F.A. should possess in order to be successful in this career?

5 Questions on the Job Description

Job description questions help the interviewer determine how much you know about the flight attendant position. A well-prepared applicant will have no post-hiring surprises, which helps reduce the airline's turnover rate. Your answers must show your ability to adapt to the unique working conditions of a flight attendant.

- **Why do you want to be a flight attendant?**

Qualities = passion customer service, safety-conscious, stressful situations, under pressure, calm head when

Here you should review all of the desirable qualities of a flight *problem solving* attendant and discuss how your strengths in these areas make you an *improvising* ideal candidate. For example, discuss how your friendliness makes you *multi-task @* eager to work in front the public, how you enjoy meeting new people *a fast paced environ.* and assisting others. Discuss your team spirit, your strong *work well* communication skills, dependability, motivation, flexibility, etc. Give *as a team* specific examples. *— Inconsistent work schedules — holidays/wkends*

- **What is the one thing you want to avoid in your next** *— flexible — adapt.* **job?** *— Relocate — Port/Span.*

I would want to avoid any position that prevents me from working directly w/ the public.

This is another type of question that attempts to make you answer negatively. Turn this negative into a positive. Explain how you want to avoid any job that prevents you from working directly with the public or requires you to work in an office all day long (with limited travel).

- **How will you handle the unpredictability of a flight attendant's schedule?**

No problem @ all.
I'm used to inconsistent work schedules
"Variety is the spice of life"

You can talk about your previous 9 to 5 routine and your eagerness to finally work in an environment that offers a lot of variety. Demonstrate your knowledge of the reserve system and explain how you look forward to the challenge and excitement of being on call. If you are single, you can mention that you do not mind working holidays and special occasions. If you are married, explain how you and your spouse (and children, if applicable) are well prepared for the unpredictability of this new period in your life.

- **How will you handle the idea of being on call with no set schedule?**

This is a variation of the above question and can be answered in a very similar fashion. You can also talk about how you will utilize your time on call (e.g., reading books, working out, etc.). Perhaps explain how this new job environment will give you more time to pursue your hobbies and interests. Do not say, however, that it will give you more time to watch TV; interviewers like people with diversified interests.

- **How do you feel about wearing a uniform at work? Complying with rules and regulations?**

Do not say anything negative about wearing a uniform. If you wore any type of uniform at school or in a previous job, speak positively about the experience. Even if a business suit was the required "uniform," show your enthusiasm for dressing that way and your outlook on dressing for success. Wearing a uniform is a sign of pride and professionalism and is well-respected by the customer. Keep in mind that by wearing a uniform, you are an extension of the company's image. Do not say anything negative about uniform standards or compliance with company rules and regulations.

- **What do you think is the most important duty of a flight attendant?** *Safety, security*

Explain that the most important duty of a flight attendant is to provide for the safety and comfort of all passengers. This involves performing and assisting with both safety and customer service-related duties. In an emergency, flight attendants must be prepared to provide direction and assistance through leadership and crew coordination in accordance with government and company regulations. As a flight attendant, you must perform your duties in a courteous and professional manner.

- **Do you know how much we pay our first-year flight attendants?**

If you have access to the information, you can talk about the airline's hourly rate, monthly minimum guarantee, normal lines, per diem, etc. If you know the airline is currently in negotiations for a new flight attendant labor contract, you can mention this as well, stressing that the pay figures you now have are subject to change. All of this information must demonstrate your understanding of the flight attendant pay system. In general, a first-year flight attendant will earn about $20,000, which increases greatly with seniority.

- **Is our pay going to be a reduction or increase from your previous salary?**

This is a question that tests your maturity level and self-discipline, especially if you will experience a pay cut. Talk about your understanding of the pay system and how you have calculated that you can afford a pay cut until scheduled raises take effect. This shows that you are a conscientious saver and have prepared yourself for this financial downturn.

- **Do you know what a probationary period is? How do you feel about it?**

Although you don't need thorough understanding of how probation and the reserve system work, you should know that you will be on call and watched closely during your early years at the airline. You should relate the probationary period to a similar rite of passage in your past. For example, perhaps you were involved in an internship where your performance was scrutinized before you were considered for a permanent position. Also, show how well prepared you are to undergo the probationary period by reminding the interviewer of your key personal traits (e.g., dependable, motivated, mature, enthusiastic, adaptable, etc.).

- **What would you consider to be the disadvantages of being a flight attendant?**

Even though you are probably aware of the negative aspects of being a flight attendant, you do not want to list them here. As far as you are concerned, there are very few disadvantages; stress how the upside far outweighs the downside. Talk about how some people are turned off by probation, the reserve system, low initial pay, etc., but how you view these as valuable learning experiences.

- **What would you consider to be the advantages of being a flight attendant?** *Serving a meaningful purpose during each flight. The feeling of accomplishment after helping people to get to their destinations safely. Through genuine customer serv.*

Review the Appendix section where we list many of the advantages of *we create loyalty and contribute to Delta's success* being a flight attendant.

- **Where would you like to be 5 to 10 years from now?** *In 5 to 10 years I see myself being the BEST F.A. that I can possibly be. Exceeding Delta's expectations.*

You should begin your answer by saying that within 5 to10 years you want to be the best flight attendant you can be, exceeding normal expectations for the job. Then say, if the right opportunity presents itself, you might consider becoming a supervisor or other member of the management team (if that is the case). *I see myself being a flight purser, an LOD f.a. and if the opportunity presents itself I would love to be a part of the*

- **Do you have any questions about this career?** *hiring and training team*

This type of question is usually asked at the close of an interview. It is *I also plan on* very appropriate and even recommended that you ask specific *volunteering* questions here. You can ask about such things as the percentage of lineholders vs. reserves at most bases, or how long you can expect to *as much* wait before a hiring decision is made. Do not ask anything about where *as I can* you might be based, how long you will be on reserve, or whether you can begin commuting to your base right away. Also, do not inquire about how soon you can apply for a supervisory position; this is too aggressive of a question for a flight attendant applicant, since you are basically asking when you can get the interviewer's job!

6 Questions on In-Flight Scenarios

Every day, flight attendants are required to make difficult decisions regarding a multitude of issues, involving passenger behavior, in-flight emergencies, and compliance with federal and company rules and regulations. The interviewer wants to know that you will be able to perform your duties under stress and consistently make good decisions. If you have flight attendant experience from a previous airline, these questions should be very easy for you; just be sure to give specific examples of your own experiences. Conversely, if you have never worked for an airline before, but have customer service experience, be sure to mention specific instances where you were able to successfully manage difficult situations with customers. In all cases, use common sense and you should not have any trouble answering these questions.

- **What would you do if a passenger were rude or obnoxious?**

Discuss how you would use your tactfulness and strong communication skills in an attempt to calm the passenger down. If the passenger continued to be rude, however, you would advise the passenger service agent (boarding the flight), the senior flight attendant or captain of the problem - allowing them to deal with the situation in accordance with company policy.

- **What would you consider to be the "ideal" passenger?**

Explain that the ideal passenger is one who complies with all safety rules and regulations onboard an aircraft, listens attentively to all announcements, is courteous to other passengers and crewmembers, and genuinely appreciates the airline's effort to provide the safest and most comfortable flight possible.

- **If a passenger came onto the airplane with too many carry-on bags and refused to check them, how would you handle it?**

You would politely advise the passenger that he or she has too many carry-on bags and that company policy and Federal Aviation Regulations only allow 1 carry-on bag per passenger. You would then tell the passenger that you would be happy to personally check the remainder of his or her bags. If the passenger still would not comply, you would then refer the passenger to the passenger service agent (if the jetway were still attached to the gate). Otherwise, you would advise the senior flight attendant or go to the cockpit and advise the captain who would handle the situation in accordance with company policy. If the passenger refused to comply with regulations, the captain might elect to return to the gate and have the passenger removed from the aircraft. Keep in mind that allowing a passenger on an airplane with too many bags is a violation of the FARs and could result in a fine.

- **If a passenger appears to be having a heart attack in-flight, how would you handle it?**

Discuss how you understand that emergency first aid training and CPR are taught during initial and recurrent training and that the aircraft has medical equipment onboard to assist in handling medical emergencies. You would advise the captain immediately of the situation and begin emergency first aid and CPR (if applicable). You also might use the onboard defibrillator in the case of a cardiac arrest. Also, explain what you know about in-flight assistance through such agencies as Medlink, where an emergency room doctor can monitor your actions in handling a patient.

- **If a passenger came onto the airplane under the influence of alcohol and was rude or obnoxious to you, how would you handle it?**

Say that you would advise the passenger service agent (if the jetway were still attached to the aircraft). If not, you would advise the senior flight attendant and/or captain. They will make a decision on how to handle the passenger in accordance with company policy.

7 Questions on Relocation

Relocation questions are very important. The interviewer wants to make sure you have no trepidation over relocation. If you indicate any type of concern over relocation or being away from home, do not expect to be called back for a return interview.

- **What base would you like most?**

The proper answer here is that you have no preference, since every domicile location offers a unique experience. If you take a mental snapshot of the airline's domicile cities before the interview, you can then talk about the many opportunities available in the various cities; after all, every city has its merits and is famous for something. If you have never really lived in a distant city, you can also explain how you are looking forward to this new experience. Whatever you do, do not say that your first domicile assignment does not matter because you plan on commuting; airlines frown on new-hires (reserves) who plan to commute.

- **What base would you like least?**

Do not offer any negative remarks about any particular domicile. As far as you are concerned, you are so enthusiastic about landing a position as a flight attendant that you are willing to work in any city the airline assigns you. Emphasize your flexibility and how you can easily adapt to virtually any situation (use specific, past examples, if possible). Another approach is to say that you understand certain bases are less appealing than others to some people, but that you are open-minded and would like to live in an area before passing judgment. As a result, you are willing to live anywhere depending on the needs of the airline.

- **Are you prepared to relocate?**

Talk about your relocation experience, time away from home in college, past business trips, etc. and how you are prepared mentally and physically for the challenge of living in a new city. Discuss how your family and friends are aware of the possibility of your relocation and how you (and they) plan to deal with it.

- **How many nights did you spend in a hotel or away from home last year?**

Include in this answer any travel you might have done, including business travel, vacations, and leisure travel. If you were not away from home very much, you can discuss how much you enjoyed the few opportunities you had to get away from home. Talk about how much you enjoy traveling, staying in hotels, and exploring different parts of the country and the world. Be specific about a particular trip, explaining why you enjoyed it so much.

- **Have you ever lived with a roommate? Did you like or dislike it?**

If you attended college, you probably spent a few years with a roommate (or two). Talk about your experiences and how you enjoyed living with someone else. Show how your friendliness and outgoing personality allowed you to get along with just about everyone. The interviewer wants to know that you are going to adjust to having a roommate while in training.

8 Questions on Reliability

Reliability is a key quality interviewers are looking for in a flight attendant applicant. A flight attendant must never be late or fail to call in sick for a trip; doing so costs an airline money and passengers a great deal of inconvenience. As a crewmember, a flight attendant must perform as a "team member" while performing his or her duties. A good flight attendant must be able to motivate other members of the team and be able to offer tactful criticism when a member is not performing properly. You should be very specific in answering these questions, sharing your past experience as a reliable person who thrives in a "team" environment.

- **What types of circumstances would make it acceptable to be tardy or to miss work?**

Explain how serious illness would be a reason to miss work, especially since it would not make sense to spread your illness to the rest of the work force; this would cost the company time and money. Other reasons would be personal tragedy such as a death in the family or jury duty. These are all acceptable reasons for missing work. As far as being late, there are very few excuses for that. If you were late in your previous job and have a legitimate story to tell about it, do so. The bottom line in the airline business is that you can never be late and must keep crew schedulers informed if you ever run late or will miss a trip due to any of the reasons cited above.

Agent taking constant breaks behind the counter. Showed that I genuinely care by asking if everything was ok. Used my psychology to let her know I noticed she wasn't performing to a high standard.

- **What would you say to a fellow flight attendant who was not working hard enough?**

The interviewer wants to know that you will take action in such a situation. Being able to recognize a weakness in the team and make the necessary adjustments (through constructive criticism) demonstrates leadership, maturity, responsibility and good motivational skills. Give an example of a real-life situation and the outcome.

Serving a 10-top within a time constraint.

- **Give an example of how you used teamwork with another worker.**

Tell a specific story about an experience where you were a member of a team working with one or more coworkers. Show how teamwork allowed you to accomplish the task more efficiently than if you had attempted to do it alone. As a flight attendant, you will constantly be working with other flight attendants where the team concept will be critical to the successful completion of the flight.

Noticed Greg struggling to communicate w/ a group of pax that didn't speak english so I stepped up + translated. Helped Greg tag bags for a large group he was checkin in.

- **Give an example of a situation where you helped a fellow employee.**

Give a specific example of a situation where you acted responsibly by helping a fellow employee. For example, perhaps you filled in for an employee whose mother was very ill or you completed a project for a worker who was out sick. Assuming other people's responsibilities shows a strong work ethic and consideration for others.

lead by example

- **How would you motivate others?**

Encouraging servers to run food

Give a specific example of a situation in which you were able to motivate others to complete a project. Interviewers like applicants who are enthusiastic and have the ability to motivate others. This creates a high degree of morale within a company. In order to do their jobs in front of the public, flight attendants must be enthusiastic and motivated about what they do.

my availability
is wide open
but if possible
would like to notify my current employer w/ a 2-weeks notice

- **If we were to make you can offer, when would you be able to start training?**

A mature, responsible applicant will answer this question honestly, stating that it is common courtesy to give a 2-week notification to his or her present employer. If you are not currently employed, "immediately" would be the correct answer here. In either case, be very specific as to the time frame. If you need a few days to get your personal affairs in order, say so. Many applicants have been turned down for the job because they could not give a specific answer to this question.

9 Questions on Self-Analysis

→ PROBLEM SOLVER

These questions allow the interviewer to measure your self-confidence (i.e., your ability to recognize your own strengths and weaknesses). Knowing your own personal attributes and limitations will be helpful in the performance of your duties as a flight attendant.

Personable
- Approachable/friendly = can strike up conversation easily

- **What are your strengths?**

- I thrive in a team environment, I'm a team player, I ♡ working w/ others to accomplish the same goal together.

When discussing your strengths, use terms that are relevant to the flight attendant position. Interviewers love to hear that applicants have a strong work ethic, are friendly, self-disciplined, work well under stress, are responsible, poised, etc. Give examples of each of your strengths (Review the desirable qualities of a flight attendant).

- Adaptable = very good at going w/ the flow + making the best of any situation. - Positive: I don't let negativity get to

- **What are your weaknesses?** *me. I'm not easily*

I get am bothered w/ a team   stressed. Great @
member doesn't perform to a high   turning a (-) into (+)
standard Turn your weaknesses into strengths or show how you are aware of
BUT I try to
motivate certain weaknesses, but have managed to overcome them. For
them,
lead example, if you are a perfectionist, explain how you realize that it is not
by
example a perfect world and sometimes perfectionism can prove to be a hindrance.

qualities/strength

- **What assets qualify you for this position?**

See "What are your strengths?" (above).

Team player
Problem solver
Approachable/personable
warm/friendly/hospitable
Poised/cool/calm/collected
Positive
Adaptable/flexible to any kind of change

- **Why should we select you for this position over some of the other candidates whom you have met?**

Here you should discuss your qualifications (in detail), stressing what you can offer the company, rather than what the company can offer you. Show how your previous experience will carry over as a definite asset to the airline. If you have previous flight attendant experience, say so. If not, stress your customer service skills. If you have second language skills, talk about these. The interviewer wants to know that you have confidence in yourself as an applicant.

- **Are you over-qualified for this position?**

The interviewer is attempting to get you to admit your over-qualification. Here you should stress that you have always wanted to pursue a career as a flight attendant and now the time appears to be right and that all of your qualifications will allow you to make a greater contribution to the airline. Explain how you have been able to use your many skills in previous professions, but would like the opportunity to work in a customer service environment with the opportunity to travel; this especially applies to older applicants who have left the corporate world to pursue a flight attendant career.

- **When you are introduced to people, what do you think their first impression is of you?**

Discuss some of the desirable flight attendant qualities and how they relate to you, showing specific examples of what people have said or would say about you. (Review desirable qualities of a flight attendant)

10 Questions on Communication

Communication is a very important part of a flight attendant's job. You must greet passengers, make announcements, and address first-class passengers by name. In addition, you must act as a problem solver, counselor, and even a psychologist, helping your passengers deal with their own personal problems. As a result, it is important for you to speak and listen effectively.

- **If a passenger came onto the airplane very upset and crying, how would you handle it?**

Show your compassion for others by saying that you would take the passenger aside and ask if there is anything you could do to help. If not, mention that you would tell the passenger that he or she may reach you at any time by depressing the flight attendant call button. Also say that you would make a point of checking on that passenger periodically throughout the flight.

- **If a passenger were obviously afraid to fly, what would you say?**

Show your ability to console passengers through communication. Ask the passenger if it is his or her first flight. If so, explain a little bit about what is going to happen, sights and sounds of the flight, etc. Also, discuss how safe it is to fly. With the captain's permission, ask if the passenger would like to see the cockpit and talk to the pilots (on the ground).

- **We exchanged introductions when you began this interview. Can you recall my name and title?**

This question is nothing more than a test of your listening skills. Many applicants are so preoccupied with making an impression on the interviewer, they do not hear the interviewer's name during the introduction. Therefore, you must make a written or mental note of the name and title of your interviewer. Not only will this allow you to answer this question and impress your interviewer, but you will also have a specific name and title for your thank-you letter. If you are not sure of the exact spelling of your interviewer's name, you can ask for it during the introduction or at the close of the interview when you thank your interviewer for his or her time.

11 Questions on Behavior (STAR Method)

One of the most common types of interview questions you will encounter during an interview is the behavioral type question. This is a question that asks you for a specific example of a situation you have been confronted with and an explanation of how you resolved it. Human resource professionals now include these types of questions in just about every type of job interview, because past problem-solving performance is a very accurate predictor of future performance in any given job. Some interviews will consist entirely of behavioral interview questions, also known as competency based questions.

You should always try to be very specific using as much detail as you can during your interview. When you are referring to an event when answering a question, be sure to be very specific and do not speak in general terms. In a few words, tell them about the situation, your task(s), what action you took specifically, and the positive result or outcome. Your answer should always contain these four steps (Situation, Task, Action, Result or "STAR") for optimum success:

serving a 10-top under a tight time constrait, under pressure, stressful,

Situation: Give an example of a situation you were involved in *team-*
volunteering to step aside to polish silverwear on a *work,*
that resulted in a favorable outcome. *busy shift when we* *commu-*
had ran out. *nication*

Task: Describe what tasks you were responsible for in that situation.

Action: Discuss all of the various actions you were involved in to complete the situation's task.

Results: End your answer by discussing the results you were able to achieve because of your actions. Before you begin the interview,

33

explain your strong points and determine how you will incorporate these points (with demonstrated STAR stories) into your answers during the interview. When answering with the STAR method, be very specific and always tell a story. Interviewers sometimes can be like psychologists. Don't be surprised if you are interrupted during your story with questions like, "Why did you feel that way?" or "What prompted you to do that? By asking these questions, the interviewer is probing to determine what qualities you have. When telling your story, it's always a good idea to use numbers. Rather than saying you were a plant foreman, say that you were a plant foreman in charge of ten people. If your story doesn't end up as you originally had planned, and the end result is not what you had hoped for, just explain that this was a learning experience for you.

Before the interview, go over your resume and think about your life experiences so that you will be ready to discuss the STAR questions you might be asked.

Example of a STAR Answer:

Situation: As a Marketing Director, I was responsible for attracting new customers.

Task: I noticed sales had dropped by at least a third over the past five years and I wanted to take action to prevent further erosion of sales.

Action: I designed a new email marketing campaign offering former customers deep discounts on our product line and met with my team to assist in preparing concepts for the mailing.

Result: With input from my team and a successful email marketing campaign to our former customers, we were able to increase sales by 25% in a one-year period.

Here are some of the most common behavioral interview questions that you may encounter during a flight attendant interview that will require answers using the STAR method.

Give an example of a situation where you had to handle a disgruntled customer and the outcome. Guest taps on my shoulder saying he hasn't been greeted in 10 mins

* Service Recovery *

Make sure your example shows how you used your strong communication skills and tactfulness to handle the customer. Do not ever suggest that you were rude or obnoxious. The interviewer wants to be reassured that you know how to handle a problem when confronted with one. In addition, it is important that your actions resulted in a satisfied customer who continued to support the company.

ot getting Sat + manager said there's nothing I can do about it.

Give an example of a situation where you were not being supported by your employer and how you handled it.

Here your example should show that you were involved in a situation where you disagreed with a company policy, but continued to abide by it. The interviewer wants to know that you were loyal to the company and would not work in violation of any policy, rule or regulation.

Give an example of a situation where you had to go the extra mile to please a customer.

This is an easy question to answer if you have worked in customer service. Find an example of a situation where you went out of your way to ensure a customer's satisfaction. Interviewers like to know that you will go above and beyond the call of duty to please a customer. In the airline business, customer satisfaction is a top priority. After all, customers equate to revenue; satisfied customers keep coming back and tell their friends about their positive flying experiences.

Here are some actual behavioral questions submitted by our members that were recently asked by airline interviewers. Some of these are variations of questions reviewed above.

- **Describe a situation in the workplace that you perceived to be unethical.** Server tries to share extra cash tip between me + him

- **Describe a situation where you initiated a new policy or procedure.** xtra glass wear at the end of each shift

- **Give an example of a situation where you had a conflict with another employee.**

- **What was the most difficult decision you had to make in the past year?** Turned down a CJO w/ another airline bcuz my ♡ is w/ Delta

- **Describe your best customer service experience.**

- **Describe your worst customer service experience.**

- **Give us an example of a situation where you had to deal with someone with a different ethnic background.** Checkin in a group of Muslim passengers not allowed to talk to women,

- **Give an example of a situation where you dealt with a problem that you were unable to resolve.** *wrong order for kid w/ allergy came out wrong twice, mom didn't want anything anymore*

- **Describe a situation in which you felt empathy.**

Note to readers: *If you have had a recent flight attendant interview and were asked any question not listed in our database, please email them to jbelotti@airlinecareer.com so that we may add them to this list.*

Situation = working at bag drop when I notice a confused passenger walking into the lobby

Task = I could tell she didn't know how to checkin so I decided to go out into the lobby to assist her

Action = I spoke spanish w/ her while processing her passport in the kiosk, converted her cash to credit, lifted her bag onto the scale to weight them, helped her move things around, brought out a plastic bag where she could put her extra items. Waited w/ her for the wheel chair assistance to arrive.

Result: she was extremely satisfied, gave me a hug, tried to give me cash, told me she didn't know what would've happened if it wasn't for my great hospitality

Appendix

Interviewing Dos and Don'ts

If you have been rejected by an airline, we recommend going over the finer details of your interview process. Try to remember everything you did and said at the interview. Were you too assertive? Did you act cocky? Were you polite at all times?

Most rejections are due to a combination of factors. In our online program for members, we go into detail about how to present yourself at an interview, how to dress, how to act and what to say. We also provide summary charts after the detailed discussion. Here is a list of interviewing dos and don'ts from our program which you should find useful before an interview or as a review tool to use after a rejection. We provide a more in-depth discussion of each of the listed items on our website.

Do arrive early. Know the exact place and time of the interview.

Do have your application completely filled out (if available) before the interview.

Do greet your interviewer by last name using proper pronunciation. Listen carefully to the name and title of your interviewer and make a mental or written note of it.

Do show enthusiasm by extending a firm handshake.

Do be aware of your posture at all times. Show confidence in your body language. Smile!

Do be a good listener.

Do make comfortable eye contact throughout the interview.

Do be factual and sincere in all of your responses.

Do bring several copies of your resume to the interview.

Do ask intelligent questions about the company and the position. Prepare these questions before the interview.

Do send a thank-you note to your interviewer

Don't sit until asked.

Don't chew gum or smoke, even while waiting for the interview.

Don't respond to questions with "yes," "no," or one word answers.

Don't make derogatory comments about previous employers, coworkers or projects.

Don't try to make the interviewer your "best friend."

Don't memorize scripted answers to questions.

Don't discuss salary, benefits, etc. unless asked to do so by the interviewer.

Don't let discouragement show if the interview is not going well.

Don't use hand gestures.

Don't discuss politics or other controversial subjects.

Don't fold your arms.

Desirable Qualities of a Flight Attendant

Airlines seek applicants who possess certain qualities that make them ideally suited for a flight attendant career. Knowledge of these qualities will make it easier for you to compose your resume and complete your application, as well as interview more successfully. Use or relate to these terms as much as possible in your resume, on your application, and during your interview(s):

* Friendly * Flexible * Mature * Outgoing * Loyal * Eloquent * Patient * Sensitive * Tactful * Honest * Poised * Decisive * Motivated * Neat * Energetic * Aware * Punctual * Responsible * Adaptable * Dependable * Intelligent*

Duties and Responsibilities of a Flight Attendant

Overall, the flight attendant position involves performing a wide range of safety and customer service-related duties. In emergency situations, flight attendants must be prepared to provide direction and assistance for both passengers and the cockpit crew in accordance with government and company regulations. In non-emergency situations, flight attendants are responsible for providing the highest level of customer service to all customers; this means always performing your duties in a courteous and professional manner.

Your primary duty as a flight attendant is to provide for the safety and comfort of all passengers onboard your flight!

Some of the most common flight attendant duties also include:

- Pushing/pulling a 200+ pound beverage cart.

- Serving drinks and/or meals to passengers aboard the aircraft.

- Maintaining a comfortable temperature in the cabin by advising the cockpit crew of any passenger discomfort.

- Communicating with the cockpit crew in accordance with company policy about any abnormal sights, sounds or situations relating to the aircraft.

- Communicating with the cockpit crew in accordance with company policy about any passenger problems including unruly passengers, medical emergencies, distressed passengers or potential hijackings.

- Keeping passengers seated and belted during periods of turbulence and adverse weather.

- Hearing and interpreting the onboard chime system, determining its origin, and responding accordingly.

- Performing mathematical calculations that are required to complete inventory sheets, convert foreign currency, count meals, provide change from in-flight sales, and verify passenger headcount.

- Using and converting the 24-hour clock for yourself and passengers (e.g., a connecting flight that departs at 13:05, departs at 1:05 pm).

- Using and converting the 3-letter airport codes for yourself and passengers (e.g., ICT is the airport code for Wichita, Kansas).

- Handling unaccompanied minors.

- Operating exits in manual and emergency mode requiring two-handed gripping, rotating and pushing of door handles and operating doors weighing up to 70 pounds.

- Assisting disabled passengers during the flight by transporting them in the in-flight wheelchair, assisting with food handling, and conducting individual safety briefings.

- Reading announcements effortlessly without prior review.

- Assessing situations quickly to determine whether to initiate emergency evacuation procedures.

- Manipulating latches, switches, knobs and controls located throughout the aircraft.

- Handling emergency medical situations including administering emergency oxygen, CPR and/or using an onboard defibrillator.

- Memorizing and knowing the location of all emergency equipment onboard each aircraft and methodically performing procedures to operate emergency equipment when necessary.

- Being prepared to evacuate a full aircraft in less than 90 seconds if necessary.

- Being able to jump onto and slide down an inflated slide.

Advantages of Being a Flight Attendant

For friendly, outgoing, and patient individuals who can tolerate these negative aspects of the job, a flight attendant career can be very rewarding. Flight attendants do work hard, but they also enjoy many extraordinary benefits. For example, as a flight attendant, you get:

- A great deal of time off (13 to 17 days off per month; roughly 6 months off per year!), up to 10 days at a time.

- Free or reduced-cost travel benefits for yourself and immediate family, covering air travel, lodging, car-rentals, and cruises.

- A lucrative benefits package, often including health and life insurance, credit union membership, employee stock options, and a 401(k) retirement plan.

- Unmatched variety - Forget the predictability of 9 to 5 cube life!

- Maximum scheduling flexibility - You are not limited to weekends off like the rest of the world!

- The opportunity to see the world.

- The opportunity to meet new people, including many celebrities.

- Independence.

- Responsibility.

- A sense of pride and accomplishment (especially when you help an unaccompanied minor or handicapped passenger safely reach their destination).

Useful Links

AirlineCareer.com website:

http://www.airlinecareer.com

Flight Attendant Free Online Prequalification Test:

http://airlinecareer.com/tests/flight-attendant-pre-qualification-test/

Flight Attendant Airport Codes Challenge:

http://airlinecareer.com/tests/airport-codes-test/

Flight Attendant 24-Hour Clock Test:

http://airlinecareer.com/tests/24-hr-clock-test/

Flight Attendant Hours and Minutes Test:

http://airlinecareer.com/tests/hours-and-minutes-test/

Flight Attendant PA Announcements:

http://airlinecareer.com/tests/pa-announcements/

Flight Attendant Dictionary:

http://airlinecareer.com/tests/flight-attendant-dictionary/

Is a Flight Attendant Career Right for You? (eBook):

http://airlinecareer.com/products/

Flight Attendant Jobs Blog:

http://blog.airlinecareer.com/

AirlineCareer.com Twitter Page:

http://twitter.com/airlinecareer

AirlineCareer.com Facebook Page:

http://www.facebook.com/pages/AirlineCareercom/150859331603035

Flight Attendant Career FAQs:

http://www.airlinecareer.com/flight-attendant-jobs/faq.htm

Boeing Aircraft:

http://www.boeing.com/commercial/

Airbus Aircraft:

http://www.airbus.com/aircraftfamilies/passengeraircraft/

Embraer Aircraft:

https://embraer.com/global/en

About the Author

Joseph Belotti is a captain for a major airline, a former US Navy pilot and a retired naval officer. Captain Belotti has been an airline industry veteran for over 40 years and has logged over 30,000 hours in his 49 year aviation career. He is a graduate of the College of the Holy Cross in Worcester, Massachusetts and holds an MBA degree from Western New England College in Wilbraham, Massachusetts. Captain Belotti is currently an Aircraft Delivery and Maintenance Test Pilot for JetBlue flying the Airbus A320 and A321 aircraft and is President and Founder of AirlineCareer.com, a website for aspiring flight attendants. He has served as an airline recruiter for both pilots and flight attendants and was a recruiter for the United States Naval Academy. Captain Belotti is also the author of "Is a Flight Attendant Career Right for You?," the second book in the "How to Become a Flight Attendant" series.

About the Publisher

AirlineCareer.com is dedicated to providing men and women of all ages and backgrounds the necessary resources to evaluate, pursue, and maintain successful flight attendant careers in the US and overseas. The site, with a member and registered user base of over 90,000 from all 50 states and 100 foreign countries, was created by a US major airline captain and flight attendant supervisors. It was launched in August, 1998 and offers individuals comprehensive information on career evaluation and step-by-step instruction on how to apply for and land a job with a major, national or regional airline. Recently, the site was recognized as one of the top aviation web sites by John A. Merry, author of 'The Aviation Internet Directory: A Guide to the 500 Best Web Sites,' published by Aviation Week/McGraw Hill.

Final Thoughts

We hope you have learned a great deal from reading *"How to Answer Flight Attendant Interview Questions."* Thank you again for your purchase. If you have time, we would appreciate it if you could post a review and share your experience with those who might be interested in our book.

Please keep in mind that the information in this publication is only a fraction of the information we offer at Airlinecareer.com, a flight attendant career website that teaches you everything you need to know about getting an airline job.

We also publish a free blog, Facebook™ and Twitter™ pages. Links to some of our services and other sites are listed on the Useful Links page. We also offer additional publications on a variety of subjects relating to the flight attendant career.

We wish you luck in your flight attendant job search and hope to see you onboard again soon!

Best Regards,

Joseph Belotti

JOSEPH BELOTTI

47387998R00034

Made in the USA
Lexington, KY
07 August 2019